Farmer Steve has a farm called
Green Hills. The farm has big hills
and trees.

1

Steve's farm has a barn. An
animal lives in it. What animal is
it? A cow!

Steve's cow and his horse eat
lots of green grass. When they eat
Steve's flowers, he chases them
away.

Steve keeps ten animals in a shed.
He feeds them each morning.
What animals are they? Hens!

The hens lay eggs.

When the eggs hatch, the animals cheep and peep. They run through the door to play in the sun.

What animals are they? Chicks!

An animal lives in a pen. She sleeps in deep mud all day. Steve feeds her corn.

What animal is it? A pig!

Steve sweeps the shed and
barn each day. He keeps his farm
neat and clean.

Each spring, Steve digs and digs.
He plants lots and lots of seeds.

He plants green beans and beets here.
He plants sweet corn there. He rakes and
pulls out weeds that grow.

Steve grows peas on three
vines on his shed wall. The peas
are green and sweet.

Steve gets his big table.

Now, he sets heaps of peas and green beans on it. He piles up beets and sweet corn.

What did Steve make? A real feast!